SIMON GRAY

Born in Hampshire, educated at Westminster School and at Universities in Canada and France before reading English at Cambridge, Simon Gray began his playwriting career in 1967 with *Wise Child* starring Alec Guinness. There followed *Dutch Uncle* (1969) directed by Peter Hall, *Butley* (1971), *Otherwise Engaged* (1975), *The Rear Column* (1978), *Close of Play* (National Theatre, 1979), *Quartermaine's Terms* (1981) and *The Common Pursuit* (1984), all six directed by Harold Pinter. More recently, *Melon* (1987), *Hidden Laughter* (1991), *Cell Mates* (1995) and *Life Support* (1997) have all played in the West End.

Simon Gray's television and film screenplays include *Death of a Teddy Bear, After Pilkington, Quartermaine's Terms, A Month in the Country, Old Flames, They Never Slept, Running Late* and *Femme Fatale.*

He has also written several novels, two radio plays and three books about the theatre, *An Unnatural Pursuit, How's That for Telling 'em, Fat Lady?* and *Fat Chance.*

By the Same Author

Plays for the Stage

Wise Child
Molly
Spoiled
Dutch Uncle
The Idiot
Butley
Otherwise Engaged
Dog Days
The Rear Column
Close of Play
Stage Struck
Quartermaine's Terms
The Common Pursuit
Melon
Hidden Laughter
The Holy Terror
Cell Mates
Simply Disconnected
Life Support
The Late Middle Classes

Books about the Stage

An Unnatural Pursuit
How's That for Telling 'em, Fat Lady?
Fat Chance

Simon Gray

JUST THE THREE OF US

NICK HERN BOOKS
London

A Nick Hern Book

Just the Three of Us first published in Great Britain in 1999
as a paperback original by Nick Hern Books Limited,
14 Larden Road, London W3 7ST

Just the Three of Us copyright © 1999 by Simon Gray

Simon Gray has asserted his moral right to be identified as
the author of this work

Cover image: adapted from *Blonde on the Spot* by Hank
Janson, reproduced in *The Mushroom Jungle* by Steve Holland,
published by Zeon Books, Westbury, Wiltshire

Typeset by Country Setting, Kingsdown, Kent CT14 8ES

Printed and bound in Great Britain by Athenaeum Press,
Gateshead NE11 0PZ

ISBN 1 85459 434 6

A CIP catalogue record for this book is available from
the British Library

For Ian Hamilton

Just the Three of Us was first presented by the Peter Hall
Company at the Theatre Royal, Windsor, on 7 October 1997,
and subsequently at Brighton, Guildford, Nottingham,
Wolverhampton, Swansea and Newcastle. The cast was as
follows:

ENID	Prunella Scales
RONNIE	Dinsdale Landen
TERRI	Carli Norris

Director Peter Hall
Designer Ti Green
Sound Designer Matt McKenzie
Lighting Designer Ben Ormerod

ACT ONE

Scene One

Late evening.

A cottage studio, with an open-plan kitchen and bathroom off. A bed on stage, a table, two chairs, one armchair, French windows opening on to balcony. Shelves crammed with books (Dickens, Tolstoy, etc.), a cassette player and various tapes and compact discs of classical music.

Hanging from the ceiling, stretching down from the highest point in a corner, is a considerable length of chain which goes through a pulley and vanishes as if leading up to the roof. The chain is not particularly noticeable. The door of the studio is open.

There is a bottle of scotch on the table. Also a bottle of dandelion wine.

ENID *is standing at the French windows. She has a glass of scotch in her hand.*

RONNIE *is walking up and down studio, agitatedly, puffing at his pipe, glass of wine in his hand.*

ENID (*coming in*). Now, what were you saying Ronnie? Oh, yes, something about your church roof, I expect, whenever I can't remember what you've been talking about it's always the church roof, people being rained on during your sermons, plaster falling into their hair – is that it?

RONNIE. No, my dear, I wasn't talking about the church roof. I was asking you if you're sure her name is Toni Gray, it seems to me it hasn't been Toni Gray until now.

ENID. Nonsense, Ronnie, she's always been Toni Gray, of course she has. (*Takes a long drink.*) For as long as I've known her.

RONNIE. But, my dear, you've never even met her. You've only talked to her once. On the telephone.

ENID. But I know her. Through and through. Indeed I do.

RONNIE. Well, be that as it may, I still don't think she's Toni Gray. Nearly but not quite. She's got a chap's name, yes, beginning with a 'T', yes – and a colour – yes, a colour – the note! Did you remember to put out the note?

ENID. Note? What note?

RONNIE. The note telling her to come down here and not to the Big House.

ENID. Yes, yes, of course I did, I must have done, I remember quite distinctly making a note to myself to put a note on – on the front – you're flustering me with all these questions, Ronnie, why are you flustering me? Why do we have to talk about it? I don't want to think about it even. It'll happen as it happens, when it happens, whatever arrangements I've made or forgotten to make, and that's all we need to know. (*Makes to pour herself another large drink.*)

RONNIE. My dear! (*Checks himself.*) Um, would you like a glass of dandelion, Mrs Price's dandelion instead – (*Picking up bottle.*)

ENID. Oh, don't be ridiculous, Ronnie! (*Pouring whisky.*)

RONNIE. But – but do you really think that that's wise?

ENID. Of course it's not wise. Wise doesn't come into it.

RONNIE. But if you're going to do this, if you're really going to do this, my dear, you're going to need a clear head.

ENID. No, I don't. I don't. A clear heart, a clear will, that's all I need.

RONNIE. Very well, my dear. (*Watches* ENID *taking another gulp of whisky, then looks at his watch.*) She'll be here any minute, I'd better get going. I'll look in – I'll look in in an hour or so. As – as planned. All right, my dear, and – and good luck or – or –

ENID. Yes, yes, in an hour. No, earlier. Half an hour! Come in *half* an hour!

RONNIE. Half an hour. Right, my dear. (*Moving to door.*)

ENID. No, no, don't go at all. Stay here, Ronnie, I may need you.

RONNIE. My dear, we agreed that this bit has to be entirely private. I can't possibly watch, I mean, I'm a vicar after all –

ENID. Well then, well then – don't watch, go in there! (*Indicating door.*)

RONNIE. What – in the lavatory! Hide in the lavatory! Really, Enid! No, no, I can't – I can't.

ENID. Ronnie, if you want me to go through with this –

RONNIE. My dear, I don't want you to go through with anything you don't want to go through with. That's been my position. Right from the very start.

ENID. Well then, if Fred wants me to go through with it –

RONNIE. Fred's position would probably be exactly the same as my position – that is, if he had any idea of what it is you're thinking of going through with. But as he doesn't, he can't be blamed for not having the position he would have if – if – he knew um –

ENID. So you're blaming *me*, is that it? Blaming me, on top of everything else. Hah!

RONNIE. No, no, of course I'm not, Enid my dear, we're not talking about blame, blame doesn't come into it –

ENID. 'Oh, Enid, Enid, I'm sinking into the marsh,' he said. 'Going straight down the tubes, into the marsh. Save me, Enid, my dearest and last hope, as always.' And he was crying when he said that, Ronnie, yes, I could see tears trembling down his cheeks. And you, Ronnie, you went down on your knees in that way you always do when you're shocked and moved – 'Oh, save him, save him yet again, Enid, I beg you. Only you can do it!' Isn't that true, Ronnie? Isn't that what you said, and what he said?

RONNIE. Well – not quite as I remember it, my dear. Certainly not in those words anyway. 'Down the tubes' possibly, because that's his usual phrase when he has a crisis – and perhaps something about a marsh, yes, I remember being struck by the marsh, not having heard it before, but as for tears and crying – no, no, I think he was his quiet matter-of-fact self, and as for me, I may have gone down on my knees but that was merely to add a little weight, there was no question of begging for him, not at all – and besides, we weren't talking about what you're thinking of doing now, we would never have dreamt of asking you to do this, good heavens, I mean a criminal act! No, no, this has nothing to do with what we were talking about, we were talking about, well, the hope that you'd return to your trusty typewriter and give Fred a new Lady –

ENID *lets out a scream, puts her hands to her ears.*

RONNIE. Sorry, my dear, sorry. I didn't mean to mention – I was just trying to explain – that there's no connection, really, between the one thing and the other.

ENID. There is a connection, indeed there is! If I'm going to be deprived of my calm, my happiness, my health itself, then Fred's going to be deprived of something too, that's only fair! And that's all I ask, tit for tat, his tit for my tat. (*Lets out a yap of laughter.*) And if you're going to deny me, Ronnie, then we can just go back to where we were. Me, to my peace and good health and he to his – his tit, as he goes down the tubes into his marsh, yes, I'll really not begrudge it to him, not at all, so you 'phone him, Ronnie, go and 'phone him –

RONNIE. My dear, my dear, please – if all this is simply about my going into the lavatory, why then – why then, of course I'll go into it.

ENID. Thank you, Ronnie. (*Calmly, then emotionally.*) You're a dear, dear man, Ronnie, I don't know what we'd do without you.

RONNIE. Thank you, my dear. I don't have to tell you how much, how very much you and Fred –

Sound of car approaching.

RONNIE. Oh, there she is! But that's – that's Fred's car!

ENID. Fred! What do you mean! He hasn't come too!

RONNIE. No, no, my dear, what are we thinking of, it can't be him – impossible. Well, I'd better – (*Hurrying towards lavatory.*) I just hope she doesn't want to use it – (*Goes into lavatory.*)

ENID (*tries to take up a dignified position, stumbles slightly*). Oh – oh, dear.

As sound of car door slamming, footsteps on gravel ENID *rushes to sink, splashes water on to her face, then unable to help herself, runs to bottle, turns away from door and gulps down scotch, as:*

TERRI *enters, briskly. She is in her mid-twenties, carrying handbag-briefcase. Sees* ENID *with her back to her.*

TERRI. Mrs Parkhurst?

ENID (*puts glass down, turns*). Yes, can I help you? Oh, you're my husband's P.G., aren't you?

TERRI. Well, his P.A. Personal Assistant.

ENID. Oh, of course. P.A. Not P.G., P.G. used to be a paying guest, and we don't have those any more, do we? But the name's Gray, isn't it? Toni Gray. Ms Toni Gray, as we have to say these days.

TERRI. Green actually, Mrs Parkhurst. Terri Green.

ENID. Ms Green, I'm so sorry. And Terri, you say. Well, we knew it was a 'T' and a colour, didn't we – (*As if to* RONNIE.) Anyway, you saw my note, that's the main thing.

TERRI. Note? What note?

ENID. Didn't I put a note on the door of the house – the Big House – saying that I'd be down here in the studio and not up there in the Big House. I'm sure I put it up because I made a note –

TERRI. Well, I didn't see any note – I didn't stop at the house, you see, because when we talked on the telephone you told me to go past it, around the bend to your studio. Actually, you said that I couldn't miss it because if I did I'd be over the cliffs onto the rocks and I'd be dead.

ENID. Oh, we wouldn't want that, would we, you down there, dead on the rocks.

They laugh together.

TERRI. But what a lovely place.

ENID. It was the bottom part of an old lighthouse, you know, I come down at all hours of the day and night, when I want to get away from the Big House and mull things over, mull them over all by myself, it's my mulling place. Mulling place. Do you have one of those?

TERRI. No – no. I wish I did.

ENID. What a nice answer. And I'm sure you will. Yes, I'm sure you will. (*Smiles at* TERRI.) Well, anyway, here you are, safe and sound, for this – this surprise business. This birthday surprise. For my husband. He's looking forward to it enormously. No, no, what am I saying, how can he be looking forward to it if I'm going to surprise him with it? Where is he at the moment, by the way, my husband?

TERRI. He's – he's in Frankfurt.

ENID. Oh yes, Frankfurt. Of course he is. Why?

TERRI. Well, he's gone to the book fair.

ENID. Is that it? – yes, I find it so difficult to follow his comings and goings at the moment. Sometimes he seems to be all over the place all at once. But why are we standing? Let's sit, shall we – and what about a drink? (*Pouring herself one.*) There's this or (*Seeing wine.*) Ronnie's daffodil – (*Shudders.*)

TERRI. Oh, no, I'd better not, thank you. Driving, you see.

ENID. Oh yes, of course you are, we heard the car, didn't we? (*As if to* RONNIE.) I mean I did, I heard the car. Did it take ages?

TERRI. An hour and a half about. To hit the middle of Dover.

ENID. An hour and a half! To hit the middle – *hit* the middle
of poor old Dover! You must have driven like a demon, my
dear. What sort of car is it?

TERRI. A Porsche.

ENID. A Porsche, I don't know about cars but it rings a bell. A
Porsche – is it blue and very expensive, like Fred's?

TERRI. Well, it is his, actually.

ENID. Oh, I see, you've got my husband's car then, have you?

TERRI. Well, it's the company car, actually. So we're allowed
to use it when – Mr Parkhurst's away.

ENID. Well, I never let him use it down here, except at
weekends when he usually comes down, not his company
car nor any other kind of car. Absolutely forbidden. We're
bicycling folk down here, go everywhere by bicycle. Or on
foot. Except when we take the train. To go to London – and
such places. And how do you get around normally, my dear,
when you haven't got my husband's company car? What
methods do you use?

TERRI. Well, I live out in Harlow so I've been taking the train
to Victoria and then the tube to Sloane Square and then a
bus to World's End. And there I am. Apart from a bit of a
walk. But there may be simpler – methods, I've only just
moved there.

ENID. What, my dear?

TERRI. I've only just moved there. Harlow.

ENID. Harlow? Moved to Harlow? Why would you do that,
my dear?

TERRI. Well, I don't know, really, come to think of it. It must
be the nomad in me, or something – but just when I'm
really settling down somewhere and making a proper little
home for myself, then I'm up and off to somewhere else
starting all over again – I mean apart from Harlow now, I've
lived in Willesden, Neasden, Ruislip, Finchley –

ENID. Hamburg, did you say?

TERRI. Hamburg? Oh, Freddie – your husband, I mean. No, Frankfurt. For the book fair.

ENID. And he doesn't take you with him? To such a seedy, sad and lonely place, Frankfurt? Doesn't he need you there?

TERRI. No, no, he needs to have me in the office. Especially when he's away.

ENID. Needs to have you in the office especially when he's away. Must be difficult for him. (*Lets out a hysterical yap.*)

TERRI. Pardon?

ENID. What, my dear?

TERRI. I thought you said something.

ENID. Oh, no. It was a yap. I do that sometimes, yap. What do you make of the moustache?

TERRI. The moustache?

ENID. Yes, the moustache. His. Fred's. His moustache. What do you make of it?

TERRI. Um, well – I – I haven't really thought about it. (*Laughs.*) But it's very – very – well, it seems to suit him.

ENID. Suit him, yes, yes, that's the secret of it, isn't it, that it just belongs there. Well, it could hardly belong anywhere else, could it, being a moustache. (*Laughs.*) He grew a beard once, you know, black and ginger, thick, black and ginger stubble is what it was really, made him look like something out of Macbeth, especially when he was drunk. Oh, how you must adore working for him, Fred, and his moustache. Tell me, what are your precise duties, my dear, as his personal – or are they all merely personal, too personal to talk about? (*Laughs.*)

TERRI. No, no, not at all. Well, I do some editorial things as well, quite a few recently, I mean recently he's asked me to look at manuscripts – oh, not the highbrow ones – the philosophy, the religions and the – the – (*Gestures.*) I'm useless for those, don't understand a word of them – but the

romantic fiction. What Freddie – (*Checks herself.*) Mr
Parkhurst calls the bread and butter *and* the jam.

ENID. Oh! bread, butter, jam. Yes. That's what romance is to
Fred, bless him, butter, jam, that's all it is, is that what it's
to you too, jam, butter, bread?

TERRI. Well, well, I absolutely love reading it myself. I mean
– I mean I'm a sort of addict. The perfect reader, Mr
Parkhurst says. If someone like me likes it, it'll make a
million. I remember the first I ever read, it was when I'd
just started working, it was by Lizzie Heartbourne, one of
her Lady Goforth's –

ENID *lets out a scream, puts her hands over her ears.*

TERRI. Mrs Parkhurst?

ENID (*checks herself, laughs*). Oh, I'm sorry, my dear, it was
just that I knew you were going to say that somehow, I just
knew it.

TERRI. Yes, well, she's so famous and brilliant, isn't she, I've
read everything she's ever written, some of them again and
again – 'Love is a Dragon', 'Oh, Heart, Oh, Heart, Oh
Hunting Heart' – and her Lady Caroline Goforth series –
'Go Forth with Courage', 'Go Forth with Hope', 'Go Forth
with Honour' – I wish she'd write another one soon, I miss
her. So does Mr Parkhurst. He says we – well, his company,
what it desperately needs right now is a new Goforth from
Lizzie Heartbourne so he can stop worrying about not being
able to pay for all his really important books. So you love
her too, do you then, Lizzie Heartbourne?

ENID. Oh well, she may have a talent for telling stories, I
suppose, but they're still tosh. Soppy tosh, that's what they
are, soppy, soppy, tosh, tosh. (*Viciously.*) I'm so glad she's
stopped. A drunken mess of a woman, Heartbourne,
revolting. But then look at me! Enid Parkhurst. Also
revolting. Quite revolting. But then we're all revolting,
aren't we, my dear?

TERRI (*after an embarrassed pause*). Well, as for the party,
the surprise party for – your husband – I've made out a sort

of provisional guest list. (*Hands list to* ENID.) And of course we have to discuss the – um – the venue.

ENID (*takes list, stares at it, unfocused*). The what?

TERRI. Well, where you want to have it.

ENID. Have what? (*Studying list.*)

TERRI. Your surprise party. For your husband's birthday, I mean.

ENID. What's this, I can't make it out, all these names –

TERRI. Well, they're everyone from the office and the agents, and some of the sales people – along with all Freddie's – Mr Parkhurst's writers.

ENID. But *she's* here, Lizzie Heartbourne! (*Glaring at* TERRI.) I've just told you how much I hate her and despise her – (*Strikes name off list.*) We want real people, real friends. The people Fred grew up with, the people who love him. Like me. Like me. His Enid. I'll be there, you know.

TERRI. Well, of course you will. But (*Awkwardly.*) I don't know any of the people from Freddie's private life. You see.

ENID. Nor do I. Not any more. (*Begins to cry.*)

There is a pause.

TERRI (*desperately*). Perhaps the best thing would be for me to go away and leave you to – to think about it and – and I'll give you a ring before – um – your husband comes back from Ham – Frankfurt, so you can think about his past –

ENID. I don't want to think – I don't want to think about Fred's past. That's the last thing I want to think about. His past. Thinking about his presence is bad enough. Present, I mean. What? What do I mean? He's not present – his absence I must mean. Yes. I – I – (*Stops, stares helplessly at* TERRI.) My dear?

TERRI (*gets up*). Well – it's been very nice to meet you, I'll be in touch before – before – he comes back. (*Goes to door.*)

ENID. Yes, yes, go away, good-bye – oh, no, no, one thing I need you to help me with – come back – come back just – just for a second, it'll only take a second –

TERRI *comes back.*

ENID. Stand there. (*Rocking slightly on her feet.*) Now – here, let me take this – (*Takes handbag from TERRI, puts it down. TERRI stands, concealing impatience.*) Now, it's this, you see – (*Lurching around her, picks up chain.*) this. You – you – how does it go, Ronnie? Oh yes, you put it around your waist – your tummy – will you do that for me – really, only a second –

RONNIE *opens bathroom door slightly, peers out, unseen by* TERRI, *as* TERRI *puts chain around her waist.*

ENID. Yes – a little tighter, I think, eh, Ronnie? Ah, that's it, perfect. Now, you see – (*Takes out of her pocket padlock, hands it to* TERRI.) if you just put this through this – and this –

TERRI *clicks padlock around her waist, stands there, patient but bewildered.*

ENID (*steps away, claps her hands*). Done it, done it! Didn't think I could do it, did you, my dear? But there, look at her! Just look at her! I've got her!

RONNIE *closes the door quietly.*

ENID *sits down, stares gloatingly at* TERRI. TERRI *stares back, bewildered. She attempts a little laugh.*

TERRI. Well, um –

ENID. How does it feel? I mean, what are you feeling?

TERRI. Well, I'm not feeling anything really except – um – that I really have to go. (*Pause.*) You did say it would only take a second.

ENID. And it did, didn't it? It did only take a second.

TERRI. Well, perhaps you could spare another second to – (*Gestures to padlock.*)

ENID. Yes, well, before we get around to all that – would you just walk to the door for me, would you do that, my dear?

TERRI, *after a slight hesitation, walks to the door, is stopped by the chain.*

ENID. Can you reach the handle?

TERRI *reaches for the handle, fails.*

TERRI. No, I can't. Mrs Park –

ENID. You haven't seen my view, please go and see my view. (*Indicating balcony.*)

TERRI *crosses the room to the balcony, is stopped before rails, by chain.*

ENID. See. Perfectly safe. I mean, even if the whole thing came crashing down you'd just hang there until we pulled you up. That's the worst that could happen. Now tell me what you see.

TERRI. Well, there's the sea and – er, and the rocks below and – and some gulls and – and the sea. (*Makes to come in.*)

ENID. No boats then? Usually there's a boat.

TERRI. Yes, well, there is one. On the horizon.

ENID. What sort of boat? (*Claps her hands.*) A schooner! Is it a schooner?

TERRI. No, it's small and black, looks more like an oil thing. Well now – (*Makes to come in again.*)

ENID. And the gulls, you know, you could watch them for ever, you'll find. So there you are, you see, you can't get out that way, (*Points to door.*) or fall out that way (*Points to balcony.*) – and there's the kitchen, you know all about that just by looking at it, and the fridge is bulging with all kinds of – everything – of course you may be a dieting person, I haven't thought about diet but you can probably make a diet by simply not eating a lot of what's in there – and – and there's the – the – (*Pointing to the door.*) oh, of course he's still in there – constipation, you see, poor dear, but, but really it's yours, it belongs to you, look, I've raised the door slightly for you so the chain can go under, you can be absolutely private, so important to feel absolutely private when he's not in there – that's it, then, I think I've covered everything, haven't I? – unless you can think of something, but we'll find out as we go along if I've forgotten – oh, clothes – you'll be worrying about those, but of course I haven't been able to do anything yet, for one thing I didn't know your size and what sort of things you like, what colours – but once we've had a good think I'll pop up to Marks and Spencer, we've got a very good one in Dover, I get most of mine from there – (*Pours herself an enormous scotch.*)

TERRI *stares at her in disbelief.*

ENID. This is my last, you know. I promised Ronnie. (*Goes to balcony, throws bottle over. As she does so.*) So good-bye, old friend.

There is a long, long pause. Then sound of bottle smashing below.

ENID. Hello, new friend. (*Raises her glass to* TERRI, *takes a vast gulp.*)

TERRI. Mrs Parkhurst –

ENID. Enid – (*Groping.*) Toni dear. Enid. Toni and Enid. (*Gesturing between the two of them.*)

TERRI. It's Terri. Terri. Terri Green. Would you mind undoing the padlock, please? I really do have to be going.

ENID. Come and sit down and we'll talk, shall we?

TERRI (*after a little pause*). Well, if you – if you just undo the padlock first.

ENID *shakes her head.*

TERRI. Enid, if I may say, I think perhaps you've had slightly too much to drink.

ENID. No, no – not slightly. A lot too much. Far too much. But no more. (*Goes to basket, takes out another half bottle.*) This *is* the last. I promise *you*, just as I promised Ronnie.

TERRI. Look, why don't you give me the key and I'll undo it.

ENID. No, no, I can't do that, can't.

TERRI. Yes, you can. Give it to me. Please.

ENID. Don't you understand, it's all arranged – the kitchen and the bathroom – and – this is your home now. Here.

TERRI. The key, please. I don't – I really don't want to make you give it to me.

ENID. You can never do that. Out of the question.

TERRI. If you don't let me have it, I'll take it from you. By force if I have to. (*Goes towards* ENID.) I mean it, Mrs Parkhurst, honestly I do. (*Grabs* ENID.) Now give it to me!

ENID. Oh dear, I've been dreading this. I do so hate violence, you know. And your face, it really is very frightening, my dear, all bunched up like a – like a – cabbage, but I can't give you the key, I truly can't.

TERRI. Yes, you can! (*Shakes her slightly.*) So give it to me!

ENID. I haven't got it, I haven't got it – oh, please don't – (*As* TERRI *continues to shake her.*) I haven't got it, it doesn't matter what you do, I can't give it to you.

TERRI (*relinquishes* ENID). What do you mean?

ENID. What I mean, my dear, is that you can search me, shake me, turn me upside down, do whatever you like, but you still won't get the key.

TERRI. Well, where is it then?

ENID. At home. Up at the Big House. In a safe place, don't worry.

TERRI. Well, go and get it then. Go on.

ENID. I can go all right – out of that door, yes. But I may choose not to come back, mayn't I? For days and days. Not come back for ever if I choose. And then what would you do?

TERRI. Somebody will come looking for me, they're bound to – Freddie will come. He knows where I am. I told him. All about the party and everything.

ENID *laughs, waves her hand dismissively.*

TERRI. He does know. I did tell him. And lots of other people.
I told lots of other people. Everyone in the office. They'll
all come looking for me.

ENID (*takes a glug of whisky*). Well, we'll see. But our own
view is – this is our view – that you're too nice and honest a
person to go blabbing out confidences about something as
precious and secret as Fred's surprise, isn't it, Ronnie?

TERRI. But when he comes back from Hamburg – Frankfurt!
Frankfurt! – and I'm not in the office – and anyway he'll be
'phoning all the time while he's away and if I'm not there
answering the 'phone and people say they don't know
where I am –

ENID. They'll be telling the truth, won't they? (*Laughs.*) They
won't know where you are, any more than Fred will. So
he'll just have to get himself a new personal – (*Gestures.*)
won't he? Very soon everyone will have forgotten that you
were there, and certainly won't wonder where you are, or
whether you're here. No. Least of all that. That's my own
view. This is my view anyway. And that's the view that
counts from your point of view. And my point of view.

TERRI. The car. They'll wonder where the car is. Freddie,
especially. He can't do without it.

ENID. Oh, how thoughtful of you, my dear, to worry. But I'm
sure there's no need. Fred will find himself another car in
no time. You know what a man of action he is when it
comes to his personal comforts. (*Yaps with laughter.*)

There is a pause.

TERRI (*attempting control*). Why are you doing this?

ENID *shakes her head vaguely.*

TERRI. There must be a reason! There must be! I know that
you're drunk but – but you've arranged it all, getting me
down here and all this – for me. Why? Please at least tell
me why.

ENID *pats the sofa.* TERRI *hesitates, goes over, sits down
beside her.*

There. That's better, isn't it? Have a little talk. What I nted.

I (*struggling for control*). Yes. Let's have a little talk. Um, you're going to tell me why.

ENID. Why? Why what?

TERRI. Why I'm here. Like this. (*Suddenly seizes chain, shakes it.*) Like this! (*Then more calmly.*) I mean, I do have a right to know, Enid, don't I? If I don't know, well then, what's the point?

ENID. I'm chained too, you see, my dear. Chained to him. Wherever I go, whatever I do, I feel the chain of my – need for him – my love for him – my loss – my loss of him. Never a moment without the chain around my heart. His heart. Connected to nothing. As it goes through some hole in the roof of my soul and out of sight. My chain. Like yours. You see.

TERRI. No, I don't see. I mean, this is a real chain and you can take it off. But I can't do anything about this chain of yours you're talking about that's around your heart and not around someone else's heart or whatever, can I? I mean, you can't blame me for your unhappiness, Enid. It isn't my fault.

There is a pause. TERRI *looks at* ENID. *Then, as if suddenly realising:*

TERRI. Unless you think I – I – Freddie and I – your husband and I are – is that it, Enid? Is that what you think?

ENID *still says nothing.*

TERRI. If it is, Enid, I promise you – believe me, please believe me – your husband and I have never ever – for one thing, I don't do that sort of thing, and anyway I've only been working for him for six months – no, no, five, just over five months – and I'm not that sort of girl – and Freddie – your husband – is not that sort of boss, he'd never take advantage and I'd never let him – and he's always saying – always – how much he loves you, how very much he loves his wife.

ENID. Always saying that, is he? Always? Well now, really, really! I can't see Fred dashing about just telling this person and that person – waiters, taxi-drivers, whoever he comes across – 'I love my wife, oh, how I love my wife!' – not his style, not my Fred's. He'd only say it when saying it would make him feel noble, not treacherous. (*Imitating Fred*.) In spite of what's happened, (*Voice throbbing*.) I love my wife, you know. I very much love, I love very much. My wife.

TERRI (*shaking her head*). No, no, the time I remember him saying it was when there was – when there was some aeroplane crash, he said, oh thank God my wife, my Enid, wasn't on that plane – and then he said, I'll never forget it because it seemed so – so true and wise – he said how dreadful it was that it took a dreadful accident to make us realise how dreadfully much we love the people we love. Like his wife. His Enid.

ENID. Plane? Where was I going? No, no, it can't have been me, I never go on planes. Though I expect they're very comfortable if you like them. Do you like them, my dear?

TERRI. No, no, Mrs Parkhurst –

ENID. Enid.

TERRI. Enid. What I'm trying to tell you – you must understand me, please – if what's troubling you – please listen to me, are you listening to me?

ENID. Yes, yes, tell me more about your life. Your romantic life. It's very thrilling, isn't it, Ronnie? (*Looking around*.) Where's he gone? Oh, still in there, well, never mind, you – you – and your romances, where were we with your romances?

TERRI. We weren't anywhere – I haven't got any romances. Look, Enid, please try to understand – I'm just a girl – I'm nobody really, just somebody who happens to work for a publisher who happens to be your husband – and I'm not even his P.G. – P.A., I mean – his real P.A.'s got six months off having a baby, so you see, I'm just a temp, that's all I am, strictly temporary, I don't think he's even noticed me –

I mean, the only romance in my life is when I go to my classes twice a week –

ENID. Classes? What classes?

TERRI. Ballroom dancing – my ballroom dancing – the only person I sleep with is my golliwog, Derek. I've slept with him since I was a baby. That's the truth, Enid.

ENID. Golliwog – didn't think we could have those any more – and there you say you've got one who sleeps with you – actually sleeps with you – and he's called Derek you say – people aren't what they ought to be, that's the trouble, that's always – always the trouble. (*Gets up, stumbles, tries to rally, looks around her.*) I used to want to dance in ballrooms. The waltz – that was one of my dreams – (*Begins to take clumsy, drunken steps, waltzing, as she drinks.*) But we were so clumsy together, his feet, you know, if only he'd let his feet flow – flow like Ronnie's – oh, what a dancer Ronnie is, aren't you, my dear – then Fred and I would have waltzed, oh, how we'd have waltzed! (*Begins to stumble.*) Oh – oh, Ronnie! Ronnie, come and get me, please! Ronnie, I need you! (*Slips down wall, collapses.*)

Door opens. RONNIE *comes out.*

TERRI, *suddenly aware of him, turns.*

RONNIE. Hello. I hope you don't mind my using your facilities.

TERRI. What?

RONNIE (*gesturing to lavatory*). I hope you don't mind.

TERRI. You mean you've been in there all this time?

RONNIE. Yes, I'm very sorry, I must have fallen asleep, I tend to do that when I'm sitting – anyway, I'm Enid's friend, Ronald Butterworth. The local vicar. And you must be the young lady from Fred's office – his P.G. isn't it, everything all right?

TERRI. Of course it's not all right, I mean, look at me! Look at this, I mean! (*Showing him chain and padlock.*)

RONNIE. Oh heavens, there's Enid! Is she all right? (*Going over to* ENID.)

TERRI. Yes, yes, she's just passed out. It's the drink.

RONNIE *picks up glass, puts it on table, goes back to* ENID, *attempts to lift her.*

RONNIE. Enid – Enid, my dear, it's Ronnie, Ronnie's here –

TERRI (*taking* RONNIE's *arm*). Would you mind getting me out of this first, please?

RONNIE. Ah.

TERRI. The key's up in the house somewhere – somewhere safe, she said. Do you know where?

RONNIE. Well, no, I don't, not really, it's a very large house, the Big House –

TERRI. Well, think!

RONNIE. Somewhere safe, well, that could be – anywhere, I suppose, probably in the snuggery, but that's a large room, and it would be a small key – a small key in the Big House in the large snuggery – um, hard to find, I think.

TERRI. Well, go and look, please, or – something to cut through – metal cutters or shears, anything like that.

RONNIE. No, I don't believe I've got – they look very sturdy, the links – no, I'm sure I haven't got anything that could –

TERRI. There must be something – some way – please! Before she comes around. (*Stares at him.*) You don't want to help me, do you?

RONNIE. Of course I do. It's just that – well, there's Enid, you see.

TERRI. I won't tell a soul, I promise I won't tell a single soul – ever! Not the police or Fred or anybody in the office. No-one. It'll be like it's never happened. Please believe me.

RONNIE. Oh, I do believe you. I really do. I can see that you're the sort of sensible and womanly, um, girl – who wouldn't want to hurt – especially someone in Enid's sort of state. You'd never want to do that, I know.

TERRI. Well then, help me, please help me to get away!

RONNIE (*after a pause*). That's simply not on, I'm afraid. Not without Enid's permission.

TERRI. Enid's permission! Her permission! Look at her! Look at her!

They look towards ENID *who grunts, gurgles, looks blankly towards them, closes her eyes.*

RONNIE (*raises his finger to his lips, lowers his voice*). Yes, I know she's – but I hope, I do hope, that soon all will be well. All manner of things shall be well. Including you.

TERRI. Is she doing this because she thinks I'm having an affair with Freddie?

RONNIE. Have you asked her that?

TERRI. Yes.

RONNIE. And what did she say?

TERRI. Nothing, nothing that made sense really. Except that there was a chain around her heart that didn't go around someone else's heart –

RONNIE. Ah. And what did you say to that?

TERRI. I told her I wasn't having an affair with Freddie. With her husband.

RONNIE. And what did she say?

TERRI. Nothing, nothing, I've told you. But I can't think of any other reason – apart from her being stark, staring mad and so she doesn't need a reason. But does she think I am? Having an affair with Freddie?

RONNIE. I really don't feel at all comfortable discussing Enid in this way, my dear. Especially in front of her – (*Gestures towards* ENID.) – with her in the room.

TERRI. It's not in front of her, she's not in the room, she's not anywhere. You've *got* to tell me. If you know why she's doing this you've got to tell me. Please.

RONNIE. Ah, well, you see, theirs has been a long, happy marriage – and she loved him – *loves* him so much, you see – so joyful their weekends up there, in the Big House together, in their snuggery, playing Scrabble, the three of us – she was so, so – well, happy and joyful –

TERRI. But it's not my fault! It's got nothing to do with me whatever's happened between her and him and you in their snuggery and your Scrabble. You must believe that.

RONNIE. Well, the issue isn't really whether I believe that – that you and Fred are having a – a thing – but whether Enid believes that you are, and whether believing that you are and doing something about it helps her to get, well, (*Thinks.*) well.

TERRI. But just because she's mad doesn't mean – I mean, you can't just allow her to do this to a completely innocent person. She should be looked after – put in a home, treatment of some sort –

RONNIE. This is her treatment, you see. Or so she thinks.

TERRI. What is?

RONNIE. You are. I expect she'll want to be your mistress.

TERRI. Mistress! She wants to be my mistress!

RONNIE. Oh – oh – in the old fashioned sense, of course, the educational sense –

TERRI. But I don't want her to be my – anything. In any sense. I refuse.

RONNIE. Well, look, there's another way of – um – looking at it, that it's – well, that it's perhaps your – (*Takes a deep breath.*) it's your Christian duty to do what you can –

TERRI. My Christian duty to be chained up – is that your idea of my Christian duty, is it really? Really?

RONNIE. Excuse me, Toni, my dear –

TERRI. Terri. My name is Terri!

RONNIE. Terri. Well, Terri, if you put it into a – well, global, religious perspective – in some countries the woman taken in – in – (*Gestures.*) – in Islam, for instance, you could be stoned to death, is I believe the case. Or flogged. Or both, even. Why, I remember only a few years back – the inhabitants of a remote Dutch village who got wind of what was going on between a young woman and a married chap, she was tied into a horse and cart and dragged around while they all lined up and pelted her with – not stones, it wasn't stones – fruit and vegetables it must have been. What I mean is – is really that with Enid, you won't be stoned or flogged, she's not even going to throw fruit and vegetables at you.

TERRI. Oh, that's nice, that's very nice – no fruit and vegetables even. No flogging, no stones, fruit and vegetables even –

RONNIE. No, no, she's very kind, she's a very kind, loving, educating woman, Enid, a natural mistress – teacher – teacher! And she needs, she does, she does, Toni, she needs your help. As her student, you see.

TERRI. I'm Terri, Terri, and why should *I* be her student, why should I help, why, why?

RONNIE. Ah, that cry – that cry that comes down to us through the ages, from Job onwards. Why me? Why *me*? But whereas we can't be specific about Job, it's all very mysterious about Job – God himself is mysterious about 'Why? Why Job?' – there isn't so much a mystery about you, my dear, as a – as a contradiction, you see. A contradiction. Because, on the one hand you say you aren't having a – a thing – with Fred. And on the other hand, other people say you are. Mmm?

TERRI. Other people? What other people?

RONNIE. Well, Fred. And Enid. And me.

TERRI. What!

RONNIE. Well, yes, Fred told both of us. You see. So that's how we both know. So I beg and beseech you, Toni, to accept your plight with Christian –

TERRI. My name is Freddie – Terri, I mean, Terri! What do you mean Freddie told you?

ENID (*waking up*). Fred – Fred – do I hear Fred – is there a Fred in the room, my Fred?

RONNIE (*getting up, going over to her*). Well, we were just talking – just talking –

ENID *stumbles to her feet precariously.*

RONNIE. Are you all right, Enid?

ENID. No Fred then? Where is he?

RONNIE. At a book fair, my dear, in – in – (*Looks at* TERRI enquiringly.) Australia, I think it is. Anyway, somewhere well and safe. Come along, come along now, up to the Big House, pop into the snuggery, then have a proper lie-down, a freshen-up. (*Helping her across room.*)

ENID. Yes, yes, lie down in snuggery, freshen up. (*Stumbling with* RONNIE*'s help towards door. Suddenly sees* TERRI, *stops.*) Who's that, then?

RONNIE. That's Fred's P.G. Remember, Enid?

ENID. Oh. Oh, yes. (*To* RONNIE.) What's she doing here?

RONNIE. She's here to help you.

ENID. Oh. Oh yes, of course. Thank you, my dear, thank you, so kind. (*To* TERRI.)

RONNIE. Come, my dear. You'll see her tomorrow, when you're better. (*Taking* ENID *off.*)

TERRI. I can't help you, I can't help you – I'm just a temp – that's all –

As RONNIE *and* ENID *go out. The door shuts.* TERRI *runs after them.*

TERRI. Just a temp! No shorthand even – (*The chain pulls her up.*) A temp.

She tries to push chain down over her hips, then up over her waist, can't. Pulls on chain, then looks around wildly. Runs to balcony, is pulled up by chain.

TERRI. Help! Help! Help!

She gives up, goes over to handbag, takes out cigarette from packet, lights it, sits down desolately.

TERRI (*whimperingly*). What do I do, I mean? I mean, what do I do now?

Lights.

Scene Two

The following morning. Bed has obviously been slept in. TERRI *is sitting, sipping coffee and smoking.*

ENID *enters, carrying a basket of flowers, spectacles hanging around her neck. She is flustered and awkward. Throughout the scene, she is a little unsteady, hungover and still slightly drunk from the day before. She stands looking at* TERRI.

ENID. Good morning, good morning – oh, you've found out how the coffee machine works, so complicated these days making coffee, isn't it – I do hope you had a proper breakfast. Yes?

TERRI *doesn't respond.*

ENID. Um, well – I brought these, they're from the garden but I can't really claim them as my own, Ronnie does all the gardening, keeps it up so beautifully – but then he loves it – (*Going to kitchen, filling vase with water, cutting off stems.*) he does the churchyard himself, you know, tends all the old graves, because he can't afford anyone – not that he'd want anyone for that, but for the maintenance, you know, and the roof – he has such trouble with the roof, always trying to raise money – these days in such a small parish and so few people about who believe in God, about nine he once counted it at, such a struggle for him, poor man – (*Stops. During the above she has brought flowers back and put them on the table.*) There – there, well, that should brighten up –

TERRI (*glares at flowers, pulls herself together*). Mrs Parkhurst –

ENID. Oh, Enid, dear. We're still Enid and Terri, you know.

TERRI. The vicar said something last night.

ENID. Ronnie, do call him Ronnie.

TERRI. Ronnie told me something last night. Something that your husband had told you. Apparently Freddie – Fred –

ENID. No, call him Freddie. That's what you've been calling him after all. Fred to us, Freddie to you.

TERRI. I don't know if you heard him – Ronnie, I mean – telling me what – Freddie – had told you. You were, um, asleep.

ENID. I know, I know, my dear, I'm so sorry. I've been wondering how to get around to – well, to apologising for my behaviour. I drank far too much, didn't I, and got a little bit out of control and falling asleep like that – it really was disgraceful, disgraceful.

TERRI. Ronnie says that Freddie told you and Ronnie that Freddie and I were having an affair. That Freddie told you that. (*Looks at* ENID.)

ENID *says nothing.*

TERRI. Did Freddie really tell you that, Enid?

ENID. Oh, my dear Terri, what is said between Fred and myself is really too private to –

TERRI. But he said it to Ronnie too.

ENID. Yes, but again, what is said between my husband and my dearest friend is private to themselves.

TERRI. But Ronnie told me.

ENID. Well, what is said between you and Ronnie is, is – I wouldn't dream of prying into it, my dear.

TERRI. But I can tell *you* what really happened between Freddie and myself, can't I? I don't know what Freddie means by saying we were having an affair – I mean I just don't understand, it isn't true. It was nothing like that. All that happened – and I mean it only happened once, I mean – it was months ago, and we were working late – I mean, we were alone in the office and he didn't have anyone else to talk to about his worries, all his financial worries, and I put my arms around him to comfort him and then suddenly we were on the sofa and – and it happened, that's what happened, that's all that happened, the way it always happens with me, and it ended the way it always ends with me, with him saying after this must never happen again, that's what he said. And you're quite right, quite right, that's when he said, 'I love my wife, you know'. And the next morning he had the sofa taken out of his office.

ENID. Sofa? I think, my dear, I really do think that what applies to Fred and me and to Ronnie and me also applies to you and Fred – more so, really, because it all seems so very, very private to you and Fred – on the sofa – and I don't want to hear, for my part I certainly don't want to hear –

TERRI (*pleadingly*). Enid – please –

ENID. – another word. Not another word. On the subject of you and Fred on the sofa.

TERRI. Well, what can I do? What do I do, I mean?

ENID (*after a little pause*). Well, let's talk about the things we can talk about. Your parents, for example.

TERRI. My parents? They're both dead.

ENID. Oh, I'm so sorry, so sorry. (*Gently.*) How did they die, my dear, may I ask that?

TERRI (*after a little pause*). In a crash. On the motorway –

ENID. Oh, dear – cars, you see, cars. And were you very, very young?

TERRI. Five. I was five.

ENID. And who – who brought you up then?

TERRI. My auntie – my auntie brought me up. Auntie Sheila.

ENID. And she was kind to you, I do hope she was.

TERRI. She didn't want me.

ENID. Didn't want you, oh dear, oh dear, all alone with an auntie who didn't want you!

TERRI (*hesitates, then as if suddenly inspired*). No, no, I wasn't alone, I've got brothers – two brothers. They'll be wondering where I am, they 'phone every evening – they're bound to come looking –

ENID. I was an only child too. I enjoyed it, being the centre of attention. But of course I was lucky enough to have parents.

TERRI. I've got brothers. I'm not an only child! And – and – I share a flat with two girls – one of them's a policeman.

ENID. Policeman? Policeman? Even if she's a man in the police, that can't be the right word for her these days, can it? Now what should one say instead? Police person – no, that doesn't sound right – Ms Plod, the police person – (*Lets out a yap.*) oh, it's really too difficult, let's just pretend she doesn't exist, shall we?

RONNIE *enters.*

RONNIE. Oh, hello, good morning, good morning –

ENID. Ronnie.

RONNIE. Um, I just popped down to find out if anyone wants anything. I'm off to the shops.

ENID. Oh Ronnie, how thoughtful, as a matter of fact I'm out of loo paper up at the Big House – you're all right for that, aren't you, my dear, as I put in six extra rolls. Oh, and some light bulbs – is there anything you can think of, my dear, that you need?

TERRI *shakes her head in a kind of disbelief.*

RONNIE (*sees cigarette in ashtray*). Oh, you're a smoker. You'll want some cigarettes, won't you? I'll pick up a packet.

ENID. Oh, better make it a carton, a couple of cartons, to save ourselves your having to peddle back and forth every time Terri runs out.

TERRI. I don't want them. I don't want anything from you. Nothing.

RONNIE. Really? Not even a packet?

TERRI *shakes her head.*

RONNIE. Are you trying to give up? I remember when Enid tried, do you remember, my dear, you made us promise to restrain you physically from going out and buying yourself – (*Realises.*) um – um – so that's loo paper, cigarettes – no, no cigarettes, light bulbs and – and light bulbs. Well then – well then – I'll look in with all that later.

ENID. Yes, yes, why don't you join us for lunch? Oh, it isn't for *me* to invite – would you mind, Ronnie dear, if Terri had lunch with us? I mean, Terri dear, if Ronnie – (*Gestures.*)

RONNIE *and* ENID *stare expectantly at* TERRI.

TERRI *squawks with laughter.*

TERRI. Oh yes, please come to lunch, please do come to lunch! I mean, why not, why not, I mean?

RONNIE. Thank you, my dear, that's very kind – and I'll bring along a bottle of Mrs Price's wine. That's a dandelion wine, you know, our Mrs Price makes –

TERRI *bursts into tears, picks up empty packet of cigarettes, gropes for a cigarette.*

RONNIE (*to* ENID). Perhaps I'd better get some cigarettes after all. (*Makes to go.*)

ENID. Oh, Ronnie – you haven't forgotten your day's main task, have you?

RONNIE. What – oh, no, my dear – but I thought this evening – or tomorrow –

ENID. I think you should do it now, my dear, and be done with it.

RONNIE (*hesitates*). Very well, my dear. (*Goes off.*)

TERRI (*who hasn't taken this in, is crying*). It's so unfair, so unfair, so unfair!

ENID *stares at her at a loss, then goes tentatively towards her.*

ENID. I know, I know, I expect it does seem like that. There must be lots of girls doing terrible things, really naughty things, and here you are, such a good girl really, I'm sure, on a chain!

TERRI (*sobbing*). If only you'd tell me how long – how long –

ENID. Are you uncomfortable then? Here, let me have a look. (*Gently pulls up* TERRI*'s shirt, exclaims.*) Oh, it is raw, isn't it? You must have done it during the night, turning and twisting, I expect, in your sleep. Lucky I thought of it. (*Going into bathroom.*) Now, where did I put it – oh yes, here it is. (*Comes out, carrying a carton from which she extracts tube.*) Now you'll be brave, I know, it'll probably sting at first – (*Puts some ointment on her finger.*) I'll be as gentle as I can – (*Moves towards* TERRI*'s waist.*)

TERRI. Leave me alone! Don't you dare touch me, don't you dare touch me!

ENID (*recoils. After a pause*). I'm sorry, so sorry, I didn't mean to – to – anyway, it's there when you want it. (*Makes to touch* TERRI *on shoulder, doesn't, goes to sit down.*)

TERRI *pulls herself together. They look at each other.*

TERRI. I'll go mad too. Then there'll be three mad people, not one of us noticing that one of us is chained. (*Pause.*) So what happens now, Enid? What do we do now, I mean?

ENID. What a good question, my dear, what a very good question. Well, for one thing, there are the books, all my favourites, which I keep here especially – and lots of lovely Mozart, Vivaldi, Beethoven – there's no Wagner, I'm afraid, not in here – he may be a towering genius, indeed I know he is, but he's quite wrong when it comes to mulling. One can't possibly mull to Wagner. But there are these – (*Taking cassettes out of her basket.*) a couple of waltzes so you can keep up your ballroom dancing, because, you see, my intention – you see what my intention is, don't you, my dear?

TERRI *shakes her head.*

ENID. We must find a way of being useful to each other. You will give me your soul. That's how you will be useful to me. I will educate it. That's how I will be useful to you.

TERRI. Educate me?

ENID. Yes, yes, put the sofa behind you. Behind us both. Our beings will surge way beyond this or that sordid sofa and on into –

There is a knock on the door.

RONNIE (*puts his head around the door*). My dear.

ENID. Yes, Ronnie, what is it?

RONNIE. May I have a word with you?

ENID. Yes?

RONNIE. Well, outside. (*To* TERRI.) Excuse us, Terri.

ENID goes half out. She and RONNIE mutter quickly together.

TERRI goes closer, attempting to listen.

ENID (*turns, comes in*). My dear, do excuse me if I take a liberty. (*Goes to* TERRI*'s handbag.*) Oh, here they are, right at the top – (*Taking out car keys.*) so I won't have to invade and forage –

TERRI. Why? What are you doing with them? Give them back, give them back – (*Goes towards* ENID.)

ENID (*as she goes out*). No, no, they belong to Fred, my dear, and he can't drive back without them – (*Exits.*)

TERRI. Freddie! Freddie, it's me, Terri, I'm in here, they've chained me up – come in, Freddie! Come in! Come in, come in – don't listen to a word they say! They're lying, they're both loony – Fred, come in, come in!

ENID (*enters*). Oh, he can't come in, my dear, he hasn't got time, he's desperate to get back to London and his work. Such a sense of responsibility, hasn't he, Fred, I hope it won't be his downfall one day. Now then – oh yes.

Congratulations, bravo, bravo, bravo. That's the message he asked me to pass on to you.

TERRI. He must have heard me, he must know I'm here! You're lying.

ENID. Lying? My dear! I never lie, and especially not to you. And of course he knows you're here, indeed he does. Hence his message of congratulations, his bravos, you see. 'Hence'. That's one of the things you'll come to understand about me, my dear. I'm a person who actually says 'hence'. You might come to say 'hence' yourself one day when –

TERRI. Congratulations, bravo's, hence – what are you talking about, what do you mean, I mean?

ENID. Oh, it's not what you mean or what I mean, it's what *he* means. And what he means is that he admires you, yes, he truly does, he does indeed, for putting that chain around yourself and padlocking yourself up so in future you abstain from sofas – *hence* his congratulations, hence his bravos, those three bravos he uttered! 'Bravo, bravo, bravo for Toni!' (*Thinks briefly.*) Terri, that is. But of course – he's sure you'll understand, my dear – office life, *his* office life has to go on, doesn't it? So he's decided to treat your moral and spiritual resignation as a professional resignation too. He's going to look for a replacement-temp immediately, but you're not to worry, no, not to worry, if he doesn't find one, as his 'permanent' is due to come back quite soon, as soon as she's delivered herself of her –

Sound of car revving up.

ENID. Ah, there he goes.

A terrible noise, followed by crashing of gears, car bumping and grinding off.

TERRI. That's never Freddie. He could never treat the car like that. Not the Porsche. You're just saying it's him to torture me.

ENID. Torture you? Is that what I've done? Oh, I'm so sorry, my dear, I certainly never meant to cause you pain, not real pain. I was just – just making a bit of a game of it, that's all. Please believe me, my dear. You're quite right, Fred isn't here, of course he isn't, it's just Ronnie, he hasn't driven for years, I don't think he's even got a driving licence and he's got to get it all the way back to London, to somewhere near Fred's office, where Fred might stumble across it – he'll be a complete wreck, poor Ronnie, anyway, I'm sure we won't be seeing him for lunch.

TERRI. And you said you never lie. Especially to me.

ENID. Yes, yes, well, I won't ever again, I promise. No more silly games, especially if they're going to cause you pain – (*Suddenly ashamed.*) oh, good heavens, there's something else – what is it? – oh yes, oh yes, of course – (*Takes package out of her basket, hands it to* TERRI, *shyly.*) I found it among some things people have been sending in to Ronnie, for his bazaar – his church roof, you know. *That* bazaar.

TERRI *opens package, takes out golliwog, stares down at it.*

ENID. There, you see. I mean, I mean, if I may borrow your favourite phrase, my dear, I mean let's forget all about you and Fred up there in London, breaking my heart, the two of you, because now the two of us, Enid and Terri, are down here in Dover, saving our souls. Souls in Dover – Dover soles – (*Yaps.*) sorry, my dear – oh, there's something I ought to tell you, as we mean to be completely honest with each other from now on, with no lies and deceits – you see, I'm Lizzie Heartbourne. Yes, Lizzie Heartbourne, creator of your beloved Lady Goforth, Queen of Romantic Tosh.

TERRI. I don't care – I don't care what sort of tosh you are, because I already know all that matters about you, you're a drunken loony, that's all you really are, that's all that matters to me! (*Throws golliwog at* ENID.)

ENID. Oh dear, oh dear, I hoped you'd be pleased that I'd confessed, but of course you're right, my dear, it doesn't matter who I am because I'm still a lush, to give me my proper name. But you see, the important thing is, I've stopped drinking. Just as I promised. That's the important

thing. Still drunk, but no longer drinking. (*Pause.*) Now.
Let's begin. With – with – it should really be the New
Testament but I took it up and forgot to bring it back down
so starting from tomorrow we'll read from the New
Testament, I've given up on getting Ronnie through it again,
he doesn't have the patience if there's a game of Scrabble or
tennis going or his blessed roof – a pity really, as he makes
the most preposterous mistakes, especially in his sermons,
blasphemous ones almost, I sometimes think it's God's will
that his roof leaks – but you'll find out, we'll find out
together how shrewd and wise and frightening, yes,
frightening, the New Testament is, and the language of it,
the language – pick up your golliwog, my dear. (*Her back
to* TERRI.) Ah, yes. (*Taking book down from shelf.*) Oh,
you'll find it so exciting, I'm so looking forward to it, and
the great thing is that as they'll be new to you, they'll
become new to me, all over again, they see so much more
than we do, hear so much more than we do, however
ordinary their ordinary non-writing selves might have been,
in fact some of them were quite unpleasant, very
disagreeable, when they were just being husbands, fathers,
wives, appalling some of them, him even, yes, I have to say
it (*Rapping book.*), even him, but no worse really than
Tolstoy or Hardy or Shakespeare, well, we don't know
about Shakespeare, except we always worry a bit about his
money-lending and then going to law to get it back – and
there are those sonnets, one or two of them – 'they that have
power to hurt and will do none, that do not do the thing they
most do show' – Sonnet 94, full of hatred and so very
personal, it really does make one's flesh and one's hair
stand up and creep, like receiving a nasty letter, a very nasty
letter – to oneself, you know, from a sort of monster – but
they could all be monsters in their different ways – although
not George Eliot, a good woman as well as a great maker,
and the poets, we mustn't neglect our poets – oh, oh, there's
one of them, Matthew Arnold, who wrote such a beautiful,
so moving – and do you know what about, my dear? This,
here, (*Pointing through window.*) our own Dover Beach –
'The sea is calm tonight, the tide is full – ah, love let us be
true to one another, For the world which seems to lie before

us' – oh, oh, but I'm trembling, I must calm down, not try to rush it all into us at once – (*Takes a breath, begins to read.*) 'Great Expectations by Charles Dickens. Chapter One. "My father's family name being Pirrip, and my Christian name Philip, my infant tongue could make of both names nothing longer or more explicit than Pip. So I called myself Pip, and came to be called Pip. I give Pirrip as my father's family name, on the authority of his tombstone and my sister – Mrs Joe Gargery, who married the blacksmith "– ' See, see, that's what I mean, tombstone, 'the authority of his tombstone'! Only Dickens, only he could find such a terrible – such a terrible phrase. An orphan. On the authority of a tombstone. Oh – (*Flustered.*) but of course you yourself, you know all about – I'm sorry, my dear, how insensitive of me, but then that's the thing, isn't it, about real books, they have a way of hurting us even as they heal us. (*Sees golliwog.*) What's he doing, still lying there, please pick him up, my dear, will you, and let us get on with our reading, please.

TERRI *doesn't move.*

ENID (*imperiously*). Pick him up, I say!

They stare at each other. TERRI hesitates, picks up golliwog.

TERRI. Well, Enid, (*Voice trembling slightly.*) here I am. Indeed, indeed I am. I mean. (*Gestures.*) So, please. I mean. Let's get on with your reading. Mistress.

ENID (*adjusts her spectacles, looks down at book, reads, her voice getting stronger*). 'As I never saw my father or my mother, and never saw any likeness of either of them (for their days were long before the days of photographs), my first fancies regarding what they were like, were unreasonably derived from their tombstones – '

She continues reading, TERRI unconsciously cradles golliwog as:

Lights.

Interval.

ACT TWO

Scene One

Two months later. It is late evening, the door is open. Golliwog is lying on pillow on bed. There are books and papers scattered about, also flowers. An exercise bike. There is waltz music on the tape-recorder. TERRI is dancing to music, humming slightly, rapt.

RONNIE *appears at the door, carrying basket, unseen by TERRI. He studies her, then knocks on the side of the door. TERRI appears not to have heard. RONNIE knocks again, clearing his throat.*

TERRI (*turns*). Oh.

RONNIE. Hello, my dear.

TERRI. Hello, Ronnie.

RONNIE. May I? (*Stepping in.*) Oh, isn't it charming – I used to enjoy a waltz myself, you know, years ago – though it's probably hard to believe. (*Begins waltzing.*) I was quite good really, though I say so myself. (*Continues to waltz, eyes shut, as if in a trance.*)

TERRI *watches him, then goes over, turns off music.*

RONNIE. Oh.

TERRI *gets on exercise bike, starts to pedal. There is a little pause.*

RONNIE. Well, how are you?

TERRI. Fine, thank you.

RONNIE. Good. As we haven't seen each other for a bit I thought I'd, well, take the liberty of inviting myself down for supper. I've brought some cold ham. And cheese. And apples. (*Putting them on table as he speaks.*) *And* of course (*Flourishing bottle.*) a bottle of our Mrs Price's dandelion wine.

TERRI. Ah. Well, I'm sorry I've already eaten.

RONNIE. Oh. What did you have?

TERRI. Omelette, asparagus.

RONNIE. Asparagus? At this time of year?

TERRI. It was tinned.

RONNIE. Ah. Well – oh, how's the chain, by the way? I expect you scarcely even notice it any more.

TERRI. Of course I notice it. It still clinks every time I move. And gets tighter and tighter –

RONNIE. Does it? Oh, well, that's perhaps because there's rather more of you to go around – and the thing about those – (*Points to exercise bike.*) I used to use one myself, you know, for a bit – is that they're only good for buttocks and leg muscles, really, they don't seem to do anything for the tummy at all. At least they didn't for mine. (*Laughs, pats his stomach.*)

TERRI *gives him a look, gets off bike, goes and lights a cigarette.*

RONNIE (*Takes out pipe*). Let's open our Mrs Price's, (*Taking bottle out of basket.*) she started making it, you know, for Mr Price when she managed to get him off the cider and the whisky – he used to turn quite violent – but now she's making him do with this, he's as calm and well-behaved as – anyway, I remember your saying you'd got to like it. Dandelions. The flavour of dandelions.

TERRI. 'Got' meaning 'had'. I *have* to like it because there's never anything else on offer.

RONNIE (*laughs*). Does that mean you want a glass or you don't want a glass? (*Looking at her.*) Shall I pour you some or shan't I pour you some?

TERRI. Whichever you like, I honestly don't mind.

RONNIE. Ah. Well then, I'll – (*Hesitates, pours, hands glass to* TERRI.)

TERRI. Thank you.

RONNIE (*sips*). Perhaps we should try something a little revolutionary – what about adding a dash of sugar – and some lemon, have you got a lemon, I didn't bring one down but I could always nip up to the vicarage –

TERRI. Oh, Ronnie!

RONNIE. What? Oh, sorry, my dear, am I being a bit irritating, often one never knows when one's irritating, except when people become irritable with one.

TERRI. No, no, Ronnie. You're just being yourself, that's all.

RONNIE. Really? Are you sure?

TERRI. Quite sure, Ronnie dear.

RONNIE. Well, that's all right then. At least I suppose it is. And if it isn't there's nothing I can do about it, really, is there?

TERRI. Not a thing. (*Smiles at him.*) Why don't you have your supper?

RONNIE. Yes – yes, I am rather peckish. (*Going towards table.*) Oh, will Enid be coming down?

TERRI. Yes, I expect so.

RONNIE. Well, I'll wait until then, she might want to join me – yes, that would be nice, I've seen so little of her, too, recently, I wonder what she's been up to.

TERRI. Oh, Ronnie, you know perfectly well what she's been up to, don't you?

RONNIE. What do you mean, my dear?

TERRI. And it'll be on your doorstep tonight, probably.

RONNIE. Mmm?

TERRI. I mean something you're expecting will be on your doorstep tonight, I believe.

RONNIE. My dear?

TERRI. Well, isn't that the tradition? Whenever Lizzie
    Heartbourne, Queen of Tosh, gets to the end of a new Go
    Forth, she leaves a copy on your doorstep.

RONNIE. Ah! So you know all about that – yes, yes, she does.
    And what a treat – so tonight. Tonight!

TERRI. It's all so silly, all this stuff about her being ashamed.
    She should be proud. It isn't a burden as she keeps calling
    it, it's a gift.

RONNIE. Oh, you're quite right, my dear, you're quite right. I
    do so agree. A gift from heaven. But it came as such a
    shock to her – well, to all of us – but of course to her
    particularly. She was just a teacher then, you see, but
    goodness, how she loved teaching – sixth form English in a
    very good school in Pudsey, no, not Pudsey, it was Putney,
    Putney. And then one day poor old Fred, well, poor young
    Fred in those days, he'd just started up on his own, putting
    out esoteric volumes on, well, anything that wouldn't sell,
    really, Turkish mysticism, rather bizarre theories about
    frogspawn and the origins of the universe – well, you know
    the sort of thing, he's still doing it, after all – and one day in
    the kitchen – I was there, I was actually there when it
    happened, well, I was always there – he suddenly gave a
    moan, a terrible, pleading moan it was, 'Oh God,' he said,
    'Oh God, I wish somebody would write a best seller for me.
    Any rubbish – any rubbish, I wouldn't be proud!' And Enid
    – Enid got up as if a button had been pushed in her, it was
    weird, mysterious – she kissed him on the head and she
    said, 'You must go away now, darling, immediately. And
    you mustn't come back until I tell you to.' And Fred just got
    up and left, as if he understood, yes, that was weird and
    mysterious too, he did understand. She went to her study
    and started rattling away on her typewriter, and then one
    morning, weeks later, she told me to 'phone Fred and say he
    could come back now. And he did. And there it was, a
    whole boxful of romance. And so Lizzie Heartbourne came
    about. And the whole ritual came about, of Fred having to
    go away and stay out of touch until she's finished. So you

see, what a landmark it's been. In all our lives. Such a
landmark. And it was such a thrill, such a relief to hear her
up and at it again that night last month, the rattle, rattle,
rattle of the old typewriter. And it's so much your doing, my
dear, the way you've settled down and accepted – and
you've had good times together, you laugh together, the
three of us have laughed together – chain or no chain – !

TERRI. Oh, it's just consequences, Ronnie, my dear, this chain
of mine. That's all. Consequences.

RONNIE. What do you mean, consequences, my – (*Stops
himself.*)

TERRI. Well, my dear, as our dear Enid said, it's there in those
books, (*Gesturing around.*) that's what they're all about, my
dear.

RONNIE. Yes, well, I suppose – well, are they all, really?
George Eliot and Thomas Hardy and Tolstoy and Dickens
and the New Testament – all of them? About consequences?

TERRI. Oh, yes, all of them. There's always this moment
when somebody does something, or doesn't do something,
like Dorothea in *Middlemarch* choosing to fall in love, yes,
choosing to fall in love with that pathetic old man just
because he's a scholar and deathly to look at so he must be
spiritual – and it's no good me thinking, oh, come off it,
Dorothea, don't be a silly cow and chuck yourself away on
him – because at the same time I understand, I really do,
because it's what she is and who she is that the terrible
things come from, misery, guilt, and in some of them,
(*Pointing to books.*) suicide – and even dead children, in
some of them. But it's their characters or their natures, in all
of them really, that bring them the consequences, and that's
what happened to me too, this – (*Plucks at chain.*) this is
my consequence. Because of my character. Do you
understand, my dear?

RONNIE. Well, yes and no, Terri. That is, in those novels I
understand it, and in general – in – in life – I understand it,
but – but in your own particular case, my dear, it was just –
well, bad luck, wasn't it, that it happened to you?

TERRI. No, Ronnie, it wasn't just bad luck. Because it didn't *happen* to me. I actually did it to myself. Wrapped it around me myself. And clicked the padlock myself. Didn't I? And I can't think of anybody I've ever met in my whole life who'd let a loony and drunken lady get her to chain herself up. Especially when being watched by a furtive sort of clergyman watching from the bathroom, and I bet you were chuckling and grunting and sucking on your pipe like always, knowing perfectly well that something – something – what word would Enid use – 'untoward', yes, 'untoward' was going to happen. Can you think of anybody but me who'd let something 'untoward' like that happen? And so since I've started reading those (*Gestures to books.*) and thinking about them and mulling (*Laughs*), yes, *mulling* them over with Eenie I've asked myself why, no, what, *what* is it in my character that got me into this chain. And do you know what I think it is, Ronnie? *Think* it is?

RONNIE (*shakes his head*). No, my – no, my –

TERRI. My politeness. I'm always too polite, too willing to please – was I smiling, Ronnie, tell me, was I smiling when Eenie told me to chain myself up. Was I smiling?

RONNIE. Well, um, yes, I believe you might have been smiling, as I now remember it. Yes.

TERRI. And was it a polite smile I was smiling?

RONNIE. You were very polite, yes, very, when you, you – almost as if you were, um, expecting it, actually.

TERRI. Like retribution, you mean.

RONNIE. Retribution. Ah. (*Ponders.*) For what?

TERRI. Oh, for lots of things, who knows what things, ever since I was a child I've been expecting retribution. I used to steal at school, you know, sweets and money and clothes, especially underwear if it was prettier than mine, but I was never caught, so the retribution could have been lying in wait all these years. And then, after all, not so long ago, I let Freddie take me. I didn't *seduce* him, or *betray* Eenie or do anything grand and sinful or even criminal, I just gave him a cuddle, and before I knew it there he was, with his trousers down and me under him on the sofa with my skirt up, being polite. And now here I am now, with my retribution. (*Shimmies.*) What's your retribution going to be?

RONNIE. Mmmm? Oh, perhaps I've already got my retribution, my dear. In my character.

TERRI. Your character? What is your character, Ronnie, my dear?

RONNIE (*laughs*). Well, just as you described me – chortling and grunting and sucking on my pipe. And – and, you see, here's the retribution, it's not just that there's me on the outside chortling and grunting and sucking on my pipe, that's what it feels like to me on the inside. Yes, yes, that's my – my retribution. Being me.

TERRI. Are you 'gay'?

RONNIE. Mmmm?

TERRI. Are you by any chance 'gay', Ronnie, my dear?

RONNIE. No. No, I don't think I am, Enid, my dear – Terri. (*Laughs.*) Terri, I mean. That's a part of the problem, perhaps. If I were gay it would give me some shape, some definition. But I've never had any strong lusts, you see. Except for food of course, and cups of tea. And this. (*Showing her bottle, pouring himself and* TERRI *more.*) And this. (*Indicating pipe.*)

TERRI. What about love then? Not lust and that, but love.

RONNIE. No, no, I don't know about love either. Apart from Enid, of course. And Fred. We were – Enid, Fred and I – in the days when Fred and Enid and I – they were such happy weekends – we played Scrabble, you know, for hours on hours, up in the snuggery at the Big House, they bought it, you know, the Big House, to be near me, in my vicarage. But that's all, that's all I know of love. And what about you, my dear?

TERRI. Oh, I don't know anything about that kind of stuff. I mean, what chance have I had, here with my retribution?

RONNIE. But still, my dear, oh, my dear, I can't believe, can't quite believe, that you're *merely* what you say you are, a smiling sort of young woman who simply accepts being chained – no, *lets* herself be chained – because, you see, I think there's more to you than you let one see, indeed I do, and that's the reason, the real reason I came down tonight. For a little chat. About the – the Stockholm business, isn't that what it's called, from what I've read and seen on television, where a lot of interdependence develops between the hostage and – and the hostage taker, in other words, are you sure you – well, you really want to be free, my dear? Because, you see, if you really wanted to be, you would be, wouldn't you? You know perfectly well that you only have to ask Enid – you've done so much for her, and you are, in your heart I know you are – a good and gentle young woman, and I know how fond you've become of Enid, but – but I don't want – I won't have her being hurt any more – look, here's the key. (*Holds it out to* TERRI.) Take it. Unlock yourself. Go. Before things get really messy –

TERRI (*ignoring key*). Go? And where would you have me go, Ronnie, my dear? I won't have a room in my flat any more, I haven't got a job –

RONNIE. A hundred pounds – (*Taking money out of wallet.*) this is a hundred pounds, it'll get you to London, and if people ask where you've been you can say you've had a breakdown, people are very sympathetic to breakdowns these days – but – but – are you sleeping together? (*Little pause.*) You and Enid? Are you?

There is a pause.

TERRI. So that's what this is all about then, is it? Poor old Ronnie. My dear.

RONNIE. Are you? Are you sleeping together? Mmm?

TERRI. What happens between Eenie and me is private to me and Eenie. At least to me. And knowing Eenie, to Eenie too.

RONNIE. My dear, I beg you – yes, on bended knees (*Kneeling.*) –

TERRI (*looks at him in amusement, struggles to repress laughter*). Oh, Ronnie, I don't want – really, I don't – (*Out of control with laughter, pulls herself together.*) Sorry, sorry, it's Mrs Price's dandelion muck – but look at you, poor Ronnie – I don't, I really don't want you to be miserable and jealous –

RONNIE. Jealous! (*Getting up.*) Of you? Oh, you silly, silly girl! You're here because of me. Because of Fred and me. Our love for Enid, Fred's and mine. It was our doing, and it was out of love. Real, grown up love.

They stand looking at each other.

RONNIE. We set out to save her. That's the whole story. In a nut-shell.

TERRI. I don't want it in a nut-shell. I want the truth, Ronnie. I've got a right to it.

RONNIE. Yes. Yes, you have. Well – well, let me try and explain then. You see, Fred's a completely faithful man by and large, bless him! He just has these momentary lapses, especially when he's desperate about his finances and thinks he's going down the tubes, which he generally is – but of course you know all that because that's what led to his, with you, on the sofa. Normally Enid would have understood. That's the way it's always gone, you see. Fred lapses, Fred confesses, Enid forgives – it's one of the foundations of their marriage. Absolute honesty from him, followed by honest absolution from her, is how Enid once put it. But this time he confessed *and* asked her to give him a new Goforth, all in the same conversation, I told him afterwards he'd made a terrible mistake, I mean absolution *or* a new Goforth, he couldn't possibly have both, but by then it was too late, she sent him away as she always does, and began her pre-Goforth drinking and breakdown, but this time, instead of homing in on a dog like the last time, that's what your chain was for originally, a dog, but thank God she started writing the day before it turned up and I managed to get it sent back without her even seeing it, a dreadful, snarling creature – or those kittens the time before that Fred and I had to have put – put into a new home – no, this time, she homed in on you. Because that was Fred's other terrible mistake. Instead of having just his normal run-of-the-mill peccadillo, some young writer he'd come across at a literary party, over and done with before she knew she'd even been begun, so to speak, he had to do it with a girl who was going to be there, every day, in his office, always a temptation, always available, that's how Enid saw it, and what was worse, there wouldn't be any more confessions, he couldn't confess about the same girl again and again, could he, so no more honesty – and in no time you'd become an obsession, far worse than kittens or dogs, and her drinking, and she was making herself so ill, so very ill. So – so – when she actually started planning to get you down here and at the end of the dog's – (*Indicates chain.*) we decided, well, I'm afraid we decided that if you were what she needed to make her well again, and to get on with a new Goforth, then she should have you. You see. But the last thing we thought would – Fred and I, I and Fred – that it would go from – from, well, sofa to chain to, well, bed. And if poor Fred should ever find out he'd be outraged, and wounded, deeply, deeply wounded, yes, wounded by the – the – sheer, the sheer – treachery of it! And knowing Fred he'd blame me. And with some justice. Because after all I'm not a vicar for nothing. Unlike Fred, I do know the difference between right and wrong. And that's where my shame is – that I should have been part in any way, do you know, when Fred saw the state the Porsche was in, the scraped paint and what I'd done to his gears, I actually thought he was going to hit me, and I yearned for him to – to – as my, yes, retribution.

TERRI. So Freddie's known where I am all along, has he?

RONNIE *nods.*

TERRI. And you helped Enid to trap me, did you?

RONNIE *nods again.*

There is a pause.

TERRI. Well, the truth of the matter, Ronnie, my dear. is that I don't care. Because I'd rather be here on the end of a chain, being educated by Eenie in my soul, yes, soul here in Dover (*Laughs.*) than anywhere else in the whole world.

RONNIE. I can't allow it, I won't, I have a duty, a Christian duty, to free you, whether you want it or not – come here, come here, out of that chain – (*Clutches* TERRI, *attempts to insert key into padlock.*)

TERRI *pulls away.* RONNIE *pursues her.*

ENID *enters, carrying typescript.*

ENID. Good heavens, what's the matter! You both look – look rather odd.

RONNIE. Really? Oh well, we're just here, sipping away at Mrs Price's dandelion and – and chatting about Dickens and George Eliot and – and our games of tennis –

TERRI. Tennis? What tennis?

RONNIE. Well, our tennis. Every morning. Before breakfast we play – Enid and I play –

ENID. Ronnie dear, (*Cutting across him.*) it's there on your doorstep.

RONNIE. Mmm? What?

ENID. Well, whatever turns up on your doorstep, from time to time, is there again. On your doorstep. The vicarage doorstep. So please go up and have a look at it.

RONNIE. I will, I will, I can't wait, can't wait. (*Makes to leave, remembers cheese.*) The cheese. (*Indicates cheese, picks it up.*) And apples. Oh, and the dandelion – no, I'll leave that for you in case you feel like a – (*Exits.*)

TERRI. Tennis, Eenie! You've been playing tennis! And with Ronnie! While I've been stuck down here –

ENID. Oh, it's only for twenty minutes or so, and it's *always* before breakfast, when you're still asleep probably, to warm me up, loosen me up, so I can get away from Enid into Lizzie and do her day's work, and it's done, she's done at last, and it's all because of you, my dear, my salvation you've turned out to be. I mean. (*Laughs.*)

TERRI. Oh, Eenie! And did you write the last bit the way you said you were going to?

ENID. I don't know. I can't remember how I said I was going to write it. I can't even remember how I've written it, really.

TERRI. Well, read it to me, Eenie. All the way from where you stopped reading last night.

ENID. Where did I stop last night?

TERRI. She's at the ball, though she doesn't really want to be, but it's a matter of pride – of honour – to show the world her independence, her freedom. Then comes all that humiliation. She runs out of the ballroom in floods of tears, then up the great steps – with everybody watching, all that titled lot, the ladies and the gentlemen, and the servants too, their eyes all fixed on her – but she can't stop, she can't compose herself. She gets out on to the parapet, then slumps against the cold wall, alone, so alone, so forsaken. That's where you stopped.

ENID (*who has been nodding through all this, turns the page, starts reading*). 'She turned her face upwards, and sobbed aloud. And then, then, then – there he was in front of her, filling the emptiness everywhere. He was reaching down, an arm was around her waist, he was pulling her up to him, away from the cold stone into his warm chest. His mouth pressed against hers. His body crushed into hers. The smell of him was the smell of the sea air, the smell of danger and safety, the smell of the man she loved. Her legs trembled, buckled, but there was no release from the ecstasy of her need. "May I have the next dance, please, Lady Goforth?" Later, as they lay naked, entwined, peaceful beyond fulfilment, he dropped a tender hand on the rich curls, the tangled love-soaked bush between her thighs and as he stroked, she – '

TERRI *lets out a yap.*

ENID. My dear?

TERRI. Sorry, Eenie, sorry, I didn't quite get the last – the last –

ENID. I'll read it again.

TERRI. No, Eenie, don't bother, just go on, keep going straight on.

ENID. There's no point in my going straight on if you don't know what I'm going straight on from, is there?

TERRI. No, right, Eenie.

ENID (*reading*). ' – the smell of the man she loved. Her legs trembled, buckled, but there was no release from the ecstasy of her need. "May I have the next dance, please, Lady Goforth?" Later, as they lay naked, entwined, peaceful beyond fulfilment, he dropped a tender hand on the rich curls, the tangled love-soaked bush between her thighs and as he stroked, she – '

    TERRI, *who has been rigid with the attempt to control laughter, suddenly explodes with it.*

    ENID *watches her, half-laughing with her but bewildered and hurt.*

TERRI. Oh, Eenie, Eenie, I'm sorry. It's just that – well, there you are looking just like you when you're reading – well, reading Jane Austen – 'Emma Woodhouse, handsome, clever and rich' – 'It is a truth universally acknowledged that a single man in possession of a large fortune must be in search of a wife' – but there were these other words coming out, very different sort of words.

ENID. Yes, very different words, aren't they? Not what you'd expect from Jane Austen or any other writer that we care for. But they're the kind of words they expect from me – even though I didn't know I'd written them. Anyway, what they sounded like. Until you laughed.

TERRI. But Eenie – Eenie, if you read it as you actually wrote it, without knowing what you'd written, I mean – here, I know how you wrote it. (*Takes typescript from her. Reads.*) 'Later, as they lay naked, entwined, peaceful beyond fulfilment, he dropped a tender hand on the rich curls, the tangled love-soaked bush between her thighs and as he stroked, she flung her head back and sobbed again. But the sobs now were sobs that came from the very pit of the sweet, invaded, precious darkness – '

ENID *lets out a scream, followed by a scream of laughter.*

TERRI, *after a second, joins in. They cling together, laughing.*

ENID. Oh, God! Oh, dear, oh dear, oh dear!

TERRI *lies, sprawled on the floor, attempting to get her breath, still laughing.*

ENID *pulls herself together.*

ENID. I've never done that before. Perhaps everybody else has, though. Perhaps all over the world people have really been turning my pages and shaking with laughter. Fred probably laughs too – and twice as much, because he sees the royalties coming in. So much to laugh at for Fred. And there's Ronnie now, up there in the vicarage at this very moment – can't you just see him, sucking on his pipe, wagging his head, great, deep chortles of laughter. And afterwards he'll just say what he always says – 'my dear, one of your best, one of your very best' – laughing away inside when he says it. Everybody laughing but me – until now. And if I'd only done it before, when I'd started – laughed at my every sentence as I wrote it – I'd have soon stopped, wouldn't I? I wouldn't have given anyone else anything to laugh at, would I? And so I'd have nothing to be ashamed of either. (*Seizes typescript from* TERRI, *throws it down, bursts into tears.*)

TERRI. Oh, Eenie, dear, dear Eenie my dear, I've told you and told you, when I was temping around London, all those dreadful offices where they didn't even see me, hence – hence, Eenie – *hence* – (*Cuddling* ENID.)

ENID *lets out a little laugh, through her tears.*

TERRI. *Hence*, I always had you in my bag, for the tube or the bus, or under the desk furtively, you kept me going, just as you keep those millions – see, Eenie? Lizzie?

ENID. You won't keep one of me in your bag any more, will you? Won't need me any more, will you? You've outgrown me.

TERRI. How can I outgrow you, Eenie, when it's you that makes me grow? Now, Eenie, no more tears. (*Goes to tape machine, puts on waltz music.*) Come on, Eenie, time for your lesson.

ENID. Oh, my dear, Terri, my dear, not yet. Not quite yet.

TERRI. Yes, yet. Quite yet. Get up. Up, I say.

ENID *gets up.*

Lights dim. They dance in the moonlight.

TERRI. Follow me – follow me – I keep telling you, follow me! That's it! (*They dance in harmony.*) Eenie, do you think you're beautiful?

ENID (*in a whisper*). No, of course I don't. Because I'm not. Not beautiful.

TERRI (*laughs*). Well, then – I think you are sometimes. Sometimes I think you're quite beautiful. Your expressions, your eyes – when you're having fun or being suddenly vague. Even when you were at your worst, sozzled and mad. More than quite beautiful actually. What about attractive? Do you find yourself attractive?

ENID. I hope I am sometimes. When it's – it's important.

TERRI. You're the most attractive person in my world.

ENID. Oh, Terri, am I really?

TERRI. But then you're the only person in my world, apart from Ronnie, and I think, I really think, indeed I do, that you're more attractive than Ronnie. (ENID *laughs.*) What about me, Eenie, do you find me attractive? (*Pause.*) Eenie? You have to answer. I'm the leader and you have to do what I say.

ENID. Well yes, yes – in some ways I – in some ways, yes. (*Little pause.*) Very. Very, very, very. Yes. (*Little pause.*) Indeed I do. Attractive.

TERRI (*swirling joyfully*). Then follow me! Follow me!

They dance towards the balcony.

TERRI. 'The sea is calm tonight. The tide is full. The moon lies fair upon the Straits. On the French coast the light gleams and is gone. The cliffs of England stand glimmering and vast' – (*Gives a little laugh.*)

ENID. 'Oh love, let us be true to one another. For the world which seems to lie before us like a land of dreams, so various, so beautiful, so new, hath really neither love, nor joy, nor light, nor certitude, nor peace, nor help for pain – ' (*Puts her head on* TERRI*'s shoulder. Taking key out of pocket.*) It's time now, isn't it?

TERRI. Yes, it's time.

ENID *unlocks padlock of* TERRI*'s chain.*

ENID. There. You're free. Free at last.

TERRI (*putting chain around* ENID*'s waist, padlocking it*). No, I'm not. And nor are you. Ever.

ENID. Ever? Oh, my dear –

They kiss.

Lights.

Scene Two

A week or so later. Morning. The room is empty. The chain goes over the rail of the balcony. Bottle of dandelion wine on table where RONNIE *left it.*

RONNIE *enters in his canonicals. He sees the chain, goes on to balcony, pulls up the chain which is attached to the golliwog's ankle. There is a knife through the golliwog's heart.* RONNIE *exhales compassionately, shakes his head. Goes over to table, picks up bottle of dandelion wine, swigs from it.*

TERRI *enters, unseen by* RONNIE, *watches him.*

RONNIE (*sees* TERRI, *starts slightly*). Just back from service. Only four of them to listen to my usual sermon, but four is a quorum, isn't it, and I did manage to get them genuinely worried about the roof, not difficult as there was that brief shower at the time – divine intervention, eh? (*Laughs. Becomes aware of bottle in his hand.*) Oh, good heavens, I'm so sorry, I hope you don't mind – sudden thirst. Quite inexplicable. There it was, you see, inviting me – temptation itself – um –

TERRI. Oh, you've very welcome, it's yours anyway and it's been there for ever, must be deeply disgusting by now.

RONNIE. Yes – yes, it is. (*Takes another swig.*) Actually she turned up, Mrs Price, just at the end of my sermon, she was in a dreadful state, patch over her eye, one of her arms in a sling –

TERRI. Where's Eenie, I was expecting Eenie.

RONNIE. Up in the Big House, on the 'phone – at least she was when I looked in a few moments, um, ago –

TERRI. She *is* coming down, isn't she? We're meant to be going to her favourite pub for lunch –

RONNIE. Oh yes, the Plough & Bucket. Stars, that is – Plough and –

TERRI. Well, did she say anything? I mean, is she coming down, or am I meant to be going up –

RONNIE. She made a kind of gesture which meant – I don't know what it meant – as I say, she was on the 'phone – but I think it meant more down than up, yes, sort of 'see you down there' –

TERRI (*lighting a cigarette*). Are you taking the opportunity for one of your little chats, Ronnie? Is that why you're here?

RONNIE. No, no – (*Showing her the golliwog.*) Why did you do this? To poor little – poor little –

TERRI. Oh well, I was remembering that New Testament bit, the not-being-a-child-any-more-and-so-putting-away-child-ish-things bit – *passage*, Eenie would call it – *passage* –

RONNIE. I don't believe He – Jesus – meant us to hang our childish things out of the – the – after we've stabbed them through the heart. No, no, he meant us to put them away in drawers, not – not – no, never – (*Unwinding chain.*) Not Jesus.

TERRI. It wasn't Jesus. It was St Paul.

RONNIE. Mmm?

TERRI. St Paul.

RONNIE. Oh yes, of course it was, how could I possibly – Corinthians 13,11 – 'When I was a child, I spake as a child, I understood as a child, I thought as a child; but when I became a man I put away childish things. For now we see through a glass darkly – ' (*Taking knife out of golliwog, putting it on table.*) There. Safe now. Almost intact again, aren't you?

TERRI. Why don't you keep him, as you're so fond of him, and after all, he's yours, really, sent in for your church bazaar, wasn't he?

RONNIE. Oh, well, thank you, my dear. (*Picks up golliwog, puts it under his arm.*) If you really have no further use – though these days it'll be hard to find a proper home – we live in such enlightened times that I really wonder if we can see anything clearly any more – except through a glass darkly – yes, you're quite right, one of my chats. Little chats. That's what I've come down for. Sorry.

TERRI. If it's to talk about me and Eenie, I won't. I simply won't, Ronnie. (*Pause.*)

RONNIE. I expect you think that I'm a weak, morally vacillating, bumbling – you know – sexless, we've already talked about, jealous, we've talked about too, um, indirectly – but the key word is weak, isn't it? That's what you think of me as? Weak?

TERRI. Well, actually, I think you're also quite demanding.

RONNIE. Yes, yes, of course, I am, aren't I? Demanding. So. So weak *and* demanding. Which means I'm also wicked, doesn't it? (*Nods.*) Wicked. (*Little pause.*) Well, anyway, I've

got to do something – something that you'll probably think
is rather wicked – look, look, there's this that I have to –

ENID (*enters*). You're still here then, are you? Oh, dear! Oh
dear, oh dear. (*Vaguely towards* TERRI.)

TERRI. Yes, he is and I've been trying to tell him I'm really
not in the mood for one of his chats, my – my dears. And
where have you been all this time, Eenie, I've been up and
down, looking for you – it was much simpler when I was
chained up, at least we always knew where one of us was.
Why can't we have a 'phone down here?

ENID. A 'phone? In my mulling room! (*To* RONNIE.) You
were meant to have finished ages ago.

RONNIE. Yes, my dear, I'm sorry, I'd forgotten it was Sunday
and I had to give the service, and then Mrs Price –

TERRI. Oh, come on, Eenie, let's be off before there's another
mix-up.

ENID. I'm sorry, my dear, I can't, it's all so hectic at the
moment, hectic. The 'phone never stops, everyone begging
me to change the title, you're right, Ronnie, as usual – 'Lady
Goforth, this is my dance' – that's the one they want –
(*Little pause.*) What I sent Ronnie down to tell you, what he
should have told you by now – Ronnie.

RONNIE. My dear, I really do think it's best if you – you –
because I've got to pop up to the vicarage, Mrs Price is
expecting me, the wretched Mr Price is back on the cider
and is behaving appallingly again, quite appallingly, beating
her and smashing up all her bottles of dandelion – (*Making
for door.*)

ENID. Ronnie, what is your reward to be when you've
discharged *all* your obligations – all of them? There is a
reward, isn't there, for you?

RONNIE *says nothing.*

ENID. Well, Ronnie? How much is he giving you?

RONNIE. Well – only a percentage, a very small percentage of
your advance and royalties, was what Fred agreed on – and

it's not *my* reward. It's for my church. My church roof. So that people, even if there are only four of them, can stand under it, my roof, protected at last from the elements, for which I thank you, Toni –

TERRI. Terri, I'm Terri.

RONNIE. – with all my heart and – yes, yes, on bended knees. (*Goes to his knees.*) It's not that I want to raise a great temple to God who may not even exist after all – no, I just want to mend my roof, the roof of a church that goes back – goes back –

ENID. Oh, get up, Ronnie. (*To* TERRI.) I don't know why he does that. They're like little fits, I suppose, and he can't help them. (*As* RONNIE *gets up.*) Very well, very well. Oh, I wish romantic Lizzie could step in here to tell us about the laughter, the tendernesses, the, yes, loving! indeed it was loving, wasn't it, my dear, we had, as we cultivated your soul together, here in Dover. But here is practical old Enid. With a cheque to hand. (*Holds her hand out to* RONNIE *who has turned away.*) Ronnie, Fred's cheque, please.

RONNIE *hands* ENID *cheque.*

ENID. Oh really, Ronnie, you might at least have put it in an envelope. (*Holding cheque towards* TERRI.) Three times your weekly wages for the ten weeks you've been away, minus so much for your board and lodging, as calculated by Fred. A cheque, my dear, for – (*Looks down at sum, hurries on.*) and you'll carry on with your reading, won't you, my dear? Promise me.

RONNIE. You'll get another job just like that. (*Snaps his fingers.*) I mean, you've shown you needn't be just a temp any more, moving from one little job to another little (*Gestures to* ENID.) job, but permanent. Yes, you could get a permanent position. In as much as anything is permanent – um – (*Lights pipe.*) these days.

TERRI (*in a whisper, to* ENID). But – but you said you loved me. And you were going to go on teaching me. You said. I mean, I mean – Eenie!

ENID (*to* RONNIE). I wish you'd remember, my dear, that it's actually the church's roof, not yours. (*To* TERRI.) I think I am, (*Nods.*) yes, think I am teaching you. This is your final lesson, you see.

TERRI. But I'm your vocation – you said so –

ENID. I think you misunderstood, my dear. My husband is my vocation, my only true vocation. And Ronnie's roof seems suddenly to be a small vocation on the side. I haven't room for anything more, you see.

TERRI. Oh, Eenie, Eenie, how could you – oh, how could you?

Little pause.

RONNIE (*to* TERRI). You must admit I tried, yes, I did try to persuade you to depart with some dignity, instead of – well, you know, this rather messy, hasn't it been – (*Sucks on his pipe again, grunts, chortles, etc.*)

TERRI (*launches herself at him, slapping him, knocking pipe out of his mouth*). Messy, messy, you're the messy, you're the messy, you're the messy, you – you – with your filthy pipe, your stench stenching up my home, fouling up my home – *my* home! (*Stops.*) This is my home. Until I choose to leave it. Which I now do. Indeed I do.

She picks up handbag, goes out.

RONNIE. Oh, a taxi, do you need a – a – ?

RONNIE puts broken pipe into wastepaper basket, still shaken.

RONNIE. I expect I deserved that.

ENID. Well, somebody certainly did, though I'm not sure – not quite sure that it was you. (*Notices cheque is still in her hand, puts it back in her pocket, looks at* RONNIE.) Ronnie dear, do you really have to keep holding on to that doll?

RONNIE. What? Oh. (*Looking down at golliwog, realising, puts it down on table.*) No, no, it can go into the bazaar, just as she – (*Sits down, pulls another pipe out of his pocket, tamps it down.*) Well, the next bazaar. Oh, dear, it's been such a – such a – far worse than the dog or the kittens that we had to – poor souls – but which one was that? Oh yes, 'A Foreigner For Breakfast'.

ENID. 'A Foreigner for Breakfast'! 'A Foreigner For Breakfast'! It was 'Stranger, Behold the Dawn', Ronnie.

RONNIE. Oh yes, yes, sorry, my dear, association of – of – but I haven't had a chance to compliment you on – on (*Realises he can't remember the title.*) – I read it with such delight, my dear, one of you best, your very, very best, I do think.

ENID. Thank you, Ronnie. (*Seeing typescript, picks it up.*) Oh, and I do hope you noticed my little tribute.

RONNIE. Tribute? Really? To me?

ENID. Page one seven three, I believe it is, at the top.

RONNIE (*takes typescript from* ENID). Page one seven three at the top. (*Finds page, reads.*) 'And your breasts, proud and pulsing mounds of passion, your arrogant nipples struggling against the soft, transparent silk – '

ENID. No, no, Ronnie, how could that possibly be a tribute to you!

RONNIE. Well, it's page one seven three, at the top –

ENID. Try page one three seven.

RONNIE (*turns pages*). Oh. Ah. Yes. (*Begins to read.*) 'No ordinary vicar, he. A man of compassion and keen, intuitive understanding, a man of the cloth, this shepherd of muscular mind – '

ENID (*interrupting*). I wonder when Fred will get here.

RONNIE. Oh, early evening. (*Brightening.*) Just in time for a game of Scrabble. (*Lighting pipe.*) The three of us again.

ENID. Scrabble. (*Unconsciously taking a few waltz steps.*) Just the three of us again! Won't that be – delicious!

Waltzes some more, as:

Lights.

Curtain.